DATE DUE

AP 2 '04		
OC 27 '04		

DEMCO 38-296

The Claude Lorrain Album

Marcel Roethlisberger

The Claude Lorrain Album *in the Norton Simon, Inc.*
Museum of Art

Los Angeles
County Museum of Art

Published in 1971
by the Los Angeles County Museum of Art
5905 Wilshire Boulevard
Los Angeles, California 90036

Library of Congress Catalog Card Number 79-158485
ISBN 0-87587-045-7

Printed in Switzerland by Conzett & Huber, Zurich

Introduction

The sixty drawings of this book were first published in 1962 under the title "The Wildenstein Album." Six years later the book was acquired by the well-known California collector Norton Simon. The drawings have so far been exhibited only once, at the California Palace of the Legion of Honor, San Francisco, in 1970 (no catalog).

Far from merely being a re-edition of the first work the text of this publication has been entirely rewritten in the light of our present knowledge of the artist. There has been a great deal of recent research on the subject of Claude's drawings. Even this author's complete catalog of 1968 has in a few places been superseded by the information from the versos and by additional insight. If the interpretation offered here is therefore different from the 1962 publication in a number of ways, especially as regards the dating, this reflects the progress resulting from a decade of study.

In 1970 the drawings were removed from the album to prevent the glue from biting further into the paper. There was no longer a reason to maintain the arbitrary sequence of the album, and therefore it has been replaced by a chronological order. The unmounting of the drawings has revealed inscriptions and sketches on the versos. Most of the verso sketches are reproduced in the appendix, and three have been photographically intensified for clearer legibility. The text itself is conceived as a practical guide to the exhibition of these drawings. It is explanatory and may best be consulted in terms of the sequence of the drawings. References to works outside this group have been kept to a minimum. Finally, the reproductions were made directly from the drawings, and the color is most accurate.

***

Claude Gellée, better known as Claude Lorrain, today needs no presentation. Born in 1600 in Lorraine, he settled as an adolescent in Rome. Except for two early sojourns in Nancy and Naples he was not to leave Rome again until his death in 1682. From *garzone* and follower of Tassi, he gradually became the leading landscape painter in Rome. He first associated with northern fellow-artists, then developed an increasingly personal, classical style. His works were in great demand; he painted chiefly for the highest Roman and international aristocracy and secured himself a comfortable fortune.

The center of his œuvre is the paintings—about 250 in number, without counting the still unknown production of his twenties. The early phase consists of lively seaports and animated pastoral views, which develop in the forties into a more serene and noble style under the impact of the Bolognese landscape. The fifties bring about the most heroic and monumental paintings with biblical or mythological themes. The late works are fewer but often large; their style is solemn, ideal, and profoundly poetic. Claude's art is concerned with the observation of nature and the idealization of it, with the rendering of light, atmosphere, and space, and with tension kept in harmonious balance.

The drawings similarly extend over his whole active life of more than fifty years, and they number today, after major losses, about 1200. Their quality and their significance within Claude's art place them among the most important graphic productions of all times. This introduction does not attempt to deal with this huge output as a whole. It does not need to because the sixty drawings of this collection sum up in a unique way the principal aspects of Claude's draftsmanship.

These drawings are more than simply a group of fine sheets such as might be gathered from the largest print rooms. They represent in a very special way the most authentic and comprehensive anthology of Claude's drawings. While this can be felt, it is not easily formulated in words; it has to do with the origin of the album, which demands some explanation.

When they first came to light in 1960, these drawings were glued into an album. It was an Italian hardcover volume bound in parchment, forty-one by twenty-nine centimeters, lettered on the spine "Disegni di Claudio Lorenese," with seventy-two pages and many interlaid endings between the pages. The sixty drawings were mounted by means of eight touches of glue along the sides. There was a title page with a portrait of Claude holding a palette, done in black chalk, inscribed "Claudio Lorenese detto Raffaello de Paesi / Nato del 1596, e morto nel 1678" (the dates are wrong). This portrait is reproduced in the 1962 edition of the album. The make-up of the volume can be dated fairly exactly around 1700. This also applies to the portrait by the same hand— perhaps that of the librarian Francesco Antonio Rensi—as the title pages of other comparable albums of the Rensi and Odescalchi collections.

The album is first cited in the manuscript death inventory of Prince Don Livio Odescalchi, nephew of Pope Innocent XI: "Altro libro in foglio coperto di carta pecora con ottant'uno disegni di Claudio Gelle Lorenese" (another book in-folio bound in vellum with eighty-one drawings by Claude). The number *81* is still inscribed at the top of the first page. The album remained in the family until it was bought in 1960 by Mr. Wildenstein. In 1957, Mr. Calmann had acquired and detached from the album eight drawings.* As far as I know, the missing thirteen drawings have not yet come to light.

While Claude had to sell his paintings for a living, he eagerly hung on to his drawings. Only a dozen or so are known to have been given away or sold by him. His death inventory lists twelve books of sketches plus the *Liber Veritatis* and a case full of loose sheets. According to his biographer Baldinucci, "five or six great books of drawings of views from nature remained to the heirs, and some bundles of loose sheets." The Odescalchi inventory of 1713 also contained an album of animal sketches (sold and dismantled in 1957) and an oblong parchment volume with 152 landscape drawings by Claude. What remains of these albums? Only one book of nature studies is still fully intact, in private hands, unpublished. The *Liber Veritatis,* Claude's chronological record of 195 paintings, in the British Museum, can also be considered intact, although the drawings have been mounted. It is natural to try to connect the Norton Simon album with the above information. Is it, or are its contents, one of the books listed by Baldinucci? Before we can answer this, it must be recalled that among the loose drawings in various collections several dozen can be shown to have belonged to about six original sketchbooks of nature drawings of various sizes (not albums with separate drawings mounted in them). One of them was a numbered book of nature drawings of which six sheets are in the group discussed here (see No. 7).

A renewed examination of the Norton Simon album clearly shows that it cannot in its form of 1960 date from Claude's lifetime. This emerges from such observations as these: it includes pages of the numbered book; the arbitrary sequence is unthinkable for the author of the drawings—in the two cases, for example, where there are two studies for one painting, the studies are separated in the album; a number of drawings have been cut down at the edge, as is revealed by the interrupted frame lines; the earliest drawing (No. 1) was carefully stuck together back to back with another sheet, then inconsiderately glued into the album; some of the sheets seem to have been mounted previously (No. 58).

On the other hand there is a secret, yet distinctive, unity in these drawings: almost every sheet is one of the finest of its kind, or a specimen without peer. This needs to be pointed out in some detail. No. 1 is, together with its back sheet, the most singular document relating to Claude's youth. No. 2 is the finest pure wash drawing from the early thirties. No. 3, with its precious date, is the finest tree drawing from its decade. The numbered sheets are outstandingly fine even among that distinguished group. Exceptional of their kind are, furthermore, the Tiber Valley in pure wash (No. 15), the pastoral composition of 1639 (No. 16), the landscape in the manner of Domenichino (No. 22), the panoramic views from Tivoli (Nos. 26, 32), the cattle study (No. 33), the heroic landscape (No. 34), the poetic Flight (No. 43), and so on, almost one by one. The thirteen figure drawings, several of which relate to the major paintings for papal and princely families, are without parallel in number and quality. This is also true of the rare, late nature drawings (Nos. 46, 53, 54). The preparatory studies for paintings are, almost without exception, particularly interesting sheets of their type (Nos. 19, 20, 23, 38, 41, 49, 51, 56, 59). The didactic drawing of Parnassus (No. 57) is a work *sui generis.*

It goes without saying that the other eleven hundred drawings by Claude include numerous masterpieces, too. But as it stands this group is characterized by the highest quality. This is all the more apparent today as the sheets, sheltered from exposure to light, have preserved a freshness and intensity of tone often missing in other drawings. We may, then, conclude that this group was selected in view of a sale by someone with access to the stock of Claude's studio. Only an intimate connoisseur of his drawings would have made a choice so varied in media, species, and period, yet so uniform in significance. In other words, the drawings must have been selected between 1682 and 1713 by one of Claude's three heirs who had lived with him—his daughter and two nephews—

perhaps in conjunction with a buyer. We still do not know if the drawings were sold directly to Prince Odescalchi or, as tradition has it, to Queen Christina (who died in 1689).**

The drawings of this collection span Claude's entire lifetime. All the media from pure wash, pure chalk, and pure pen to mixed techniques and colored ground are represented. Likewise, examples of the various types of drawings are found. There are about twenty-three studies from nature, thirteen preparatory sheets for paintings, the same number of figure drawings, and eleven autonomous images. The relative distribution of these categories reflects fairly accurately Claude's overall production, except that there are more figure drawings here. It remains for us to trace with a few brief remarks the evolution of Claude's draftsmanship as it unfolds before our eyes in the sequence of this collection.

The young Claude found his style rather hesitantly. His production of the twenties, which must have consisted of numerous brashly done paintings, blends with the largely anonymous output of the school of Tassi, as seen in the first item of this collection. What was to elevate Claude above his precursors was his systematic study of nature from which his whole art draws its lasting truth. It has long been realized that the plein-air studies from his early maturity are the most brilliant achievement of his draftsmanship. From the thirties and early forties date several hundred nature views done in the Roman Campagna with infinite variety of technique and type. This collection contains an especially rich display of them (between Nos. 2 and 17). They are, simultaneously, spontaneous and composed, casual and objective, exuberant and controlled, sketchy and thorough, descriptive and stylized. Their surface unity accords with the illusion of depth; compact forms are set against empty forms; foreground matches distance; light responds to shadow; orthogonals

contend with diagonals. The structure of these drawings consists of boldly interlocking forms which complement and contrast with each other in tension and equilibrium. Some of the formal relationships are described in the individual catalog entries.

The nature drawings usually consist of two or three clearly separated planes within a rather closed space. The foreground is often dark, with strong framing accents. One side may show a regular spatial progression, whereas the other may on the contrary suggest depth by abrupt contrasts (No. 11). Several drawings have the same underlying pattern yet differ widely in their effect (Nos. 7, 11, 54). However lifelike the views appear, the details are actually few. The multitude of nature is simplified into large, sometimes almost abstract, forms which are adapted to basic geometric shapes and regular outlines. This purity of vision, favored by the clear Italian light, clearly distinguishes Claude's art from Dutch landscapes of the time. Hand in hand with it goes the purity of the technical means, above all Claude's mastery of the wash which has been imitated ever since.

But the formal aspect of Claude's nature drawings is never an end in itself. It is the vehicle for the evocation of a peaceful, poetic feeling for nature which has its roots far back in ancient literature.

The study of nature and the composition of a painting represented for Claude two outwardly separate realms. He did not apply his nature views directly to the painted work. While the former always register one particular site or object, his paintings create a complex synthesis which transposes the accidental phenomena of nature into the domain of the ideal. After their peak in the years around 1640, nature drawings are gradually replaced by studies for paintings. The few late nature drawings differ in their restraint and individuality from the grand style of the earlier ones. The preliminary drawings, on the other hand, become ever more numerous—they outnumber nature drawings two to one—and Claude must have spent far more time on their detailed elaboration, which usually combines pen and wash. By definition, they refer to another work in a different medium—the painting for which they prepare and with which they ought to be compared. To us the most fascinating examples of the studies are those in which we can directly participate in the searching act of creation, as in Nos. 19f., 41, 49, 51. The spatial layout of the preparatory works depends on the size of the projected painting; the fabric of their motifs and their mood express in a subtle equivalence the essence of the literary or biblical topic of the painting.

Claude's landscapes are always the setting for a human theme. If the pastoral scenes of the early phase are tied to convention, the subjects later gain in importance, and they condition the entire form of a painting. Claude's figure drawings have to be seen in this context, which also accounts for the presence of an unusual number of them in this collection. From an academic viewpoint, they may not measure up to Carracci's or Reni's figure studies. On canvas, the figures of Claude are at times better designed. Their importance for the artist as the focus of a whole painting is the reason for the elaborate quality of these drawings. Most of them were done as advanced studies while the canvas was in progress; some are records of particularly important groups (Nos. 39, 57); others astonish for their pictorial or coloristic features (Nos. 35, 37).

In connection with Claude, the word "study" does not imply a mere working step in the progression towards a final solution, which was the function of most of Carracci's or Poussin's drawings. On the contrary, Claude throughout his life stressed the pictorial autonomy of his drawings. Even the trial sketch is carried out beyond its immediate goal into a finished image. He completes the figure sketch with surrounding motifs into an independent substitute for a painting. He makes the nature study into a final, framed work that could be hung on the wall. And a whole group of his finest drawings, mostly dating from his mature years, forms a class of autonomous "tableaux dessinés"—here e.g. Nos. 16, 33f., 40, 58. They do not relate to other works; they have a penetrating execution and show a narrow composition proper to the size of a drawing. In type, they lead back to the Flemish masters active around 1600 and to the gouaches of Elsheimer. In essence, they sum up Claude's attitude towards drawing as the realm of complete images on a small scale, each having the character of a final work of art. The application of this concept throughout his life, together with his artistic subtlety and inventiveness, conveys to his graphic œuvre its unique weight.

* (see page 6) An early pen drawing of a villa (no. 56 of the complete catalog), a chalk landscape from the numbered album, ca. 1640 (471), a landscape composition (584), a figure drawing of LV 134 on parchment (754), a figure drawing ca. 1658 (812), two wash landscapes (one dated 1663; 906f.), and a study for LV 185, from ca. 1672 (1079).

** (see page 8) Further details about the drawing books and the early provenance of Claude's drawings will be found in the complete catalog, 1968, pp. 55–69.

Bibliography

W   followed by a catalog number (plate number) refers to my first edition of these drawings: *Claude Lorrain, The Wildenstein Album,* Paris (Les Beaux-Arts) 1962. French edition *Claude Lorrain, L'Album Wildenstein, ibid.*

D   followed by a catalog number (plate number) refers to my complete catalog of Claude's drawings, in which further literature for the individual items may be found: *Claude Lorrain, The Drawings,* 2 vols., Berkeley and Los Angeles (University of California Press) 1968.

No. refers to the numbers (plates) of the present catalog. Any literature after 1968 is also quoted.

LV refers to the *Liber Veritatis* in the British Museum, which is Claude's chronological book of records drawn after his completed paintings. The paintings are grouped together in my *Claude Lorrain, The Paintings,* 2 vols., New Haven (Yale University Press) 1961.

Pen implies brown ink, unless otherwise stated. The dimensions refer to the sheet, not to the frame lines. Most drawings are prepared by a black chalk underdrawing which may be nearly invisible.

Catalog

1 *A Shipyard*

213 × 320 mm. Pen, light brown wash. Has suffered and is stained. Glued together most awkwardly along irregular edges with another sheet which bears a gray chalk drawing of a lady on horseback with hounds (Pl. 64). The presence of this couple of drawings, the only enigmatic ones in the album, puts the question of attribution into a special light. Claude himself must have saved them as records of his artistic beginnings. But no further progress beyond what has been said to date is as yet possible. A detailed discussion will be found in the literature cited below.

A Shipyard, a painstakingly precise drawing partly carried out with the ruler, corresponds to and probably copies a large, more extended painting in Rumanian private hands. Drawing and painting belong to the circle of Tassi and precisely, it seems, to Filippo Napoletano, on whom see now Salerno, in *Storia dell'Arte* 6, 1971. A few other drawings of ships are by the same hand. Whether or not this is a drawing by Claude from the (early) twenties remains a question. It is the sort of work he may be expected to have done. His few known studies with ships are admittedly altogether different; on the other hand the tiny mannerist figures of this sheet are the exact precursors of those appearing in drawings by Claude from 1630 (D 46).

The mounted lady on the verso is a copy after a detail of a large painting done between 1638 and 1641 by Claude Deruet, whose assistant Claude had been in Nancy, 1625–27. Although conceivably the motif already existed earlier in Deruet's œuvre, the technique excludes Deruet's authorship of the drawing. Was it sent to Claude from Deruet's studio, or is it his own copy? The circumstances escape us. Except for Claude's taste for courtly figures, no further link with Deruet can be ascertained in his œuvre. However, I continue to see in the chalk stroke of this sheet the hand of Claude from ca. 1640 (compare Nos. 23, 29). In conclusion, I think that both sides are very likely the work of Claude.

W 33. D 331, 1193. Roethlisberger, in *National Gallery of Art, Report and Studies 1969,* Washington 1970, 40. Kitson's recent rejection (*Master Drawings* VIII, No. 4) of the "Deruet" makes no sense.

2 A Ruin on the Palatine

200 × 269 mm. Brown and brown-gray wash. Watermark: fleur-de-lis in an oval. Date: 1630–35.

The ruins of ancient Rome, which had been drawn by artists for a century, belong to the repertoire of Claude's early drawings and paintings. He was soon to abandon their study, and the ruins of his mature paintings are for the most part imaginary. This sheet is the finest of his early nature studies with ruins. Surprisingly, the building does not belong to the set of famous antique vestiges. I am indebted to W. L. MacDonald for identifying it as the still extant, but now more dilapidated Castellum Aquae on the Palatine. The handling already reveals Claude's sovereign mastery of the pure wash medium. Deep spots of wash shape the volume of the bulky building, while all other areas are rendered in transparent tonal surfaces. The outlines of the forms are accentuated with a pointed brush which still echoes the draftsmanship of Breenbergh and of Filippo Napoletano (see Longhi, in *Paragone* 95, 1957, Pl. 34). The central mass is flanked by a diagonal repoussoir on the left, by rectangular surfaces of contrasting tone on the right (wall and pine trees), with two figures indicating the scale.

The verso shows six compartments, two with outline sketches of extended landscapes in red chalk, too faint to be reproduced. One is a river view with trees on the right and a hill in the center (comparable to D 62v, 95v, 165v).

W 36. D 71.

3 A Group of Trees in Sunlight

248 × 190 mm. Pen, brown wash. The pen frame remains only on the left side. Inscribed on the verso *Claude Ge/fecit Roma 1633*.

Although our knowledge of Claude's early years is fragmentary, it does not seem chance that this is the only nature drawing to be signed and dated before the mid-thirties. Among his many tree studies of the time, this is indeed the most splendid. To Claude trees were the motif par excellence of nature (having for him the meaning the figure had for the history painter). He drew them with infinite variety. Here, the curly penwork has a uniform finesse characteristic of his early maturity. But it is the wash, laid on sparingly in flat touches, which gives shape to the mass of foliage, causing

the viewer the sensation of deep shadows and of sunlight in a lively interaction. Below and on the left, some minimal indications of the surroundings create the illusion of a pictorial space. The bottom zone, rendered as a plain wash surface charged with color along the sloping edge, contrasts with the vibrating foliage. The white area behind, limited by a single pen outline, reads as a distant hill. The date on this drawing is a precious keystone for the chronology of Claude's nature studies.

W 12. D 63.

4 View of Rome from Sta. Croce in Gerusalemme

183 × 264 mm. Black chalk. Date: ca. 1638.

This is one of the very few panoramic urban views by Claude. Not a topographer, he would draw and paint individual ruins or views in the country, but rarely cityscapes. Even when he turns to the city, his intent is not to describe the maze of houses and roofs. Here, a few large buildings and ruins stand out in the foreground, whereas the distance is rendred as a homogeneous zone. Though open on the sides and unassuming, the view is symmetrically arranged. In the center is the apse of the ancient church of Sta. Croce in Gerusalemme, one of the seven stations of Rome, as it looked before the complete remodeling in the eighteenth century (the campanile still stands unaltered). Immediately to the right are the ruins of the ancient Sessorium, to the left those of the Amphitheatrum Castrense. Looking westward in the direction of the city one can make out in the distance, starting from the bell tower, the dome of SS. Marcellino e Pietro, the Colosseum, the Senate's palace, and the cupola of St. Peter's at the extreme right. The area is nowadays totally overbuilt. The illusion of depth is given by the contrast of scale between the church and the distance. The stylistic unity results from the regularity of the stroke and from the interaction of dominating horizontals and short verticals. The handling compares with chalk drawings from the Tivoli book (Nos. 8, 9). As in several other nature drawings of the thirties, the sheet contains two sketches. The second one is an extensive view in the Campagna, done with a few broad chalk lines.

W 21. D 449.

5 *Pastoral Landscape Composition*

210 × 275 mm. Black chalk, light gray wash, a touch of brown wash at the upper right, heightened in three spots for deleting stains; pen frame. Date: ca. 1638–40.

Except for the first drawing, this sheet, affected by foxing, is the only one of the album to have lost some of its freshness. It is one of the few compositions done essentially in chalk. The setting and the motifs are those occurring in paintings of his early maturity. The careful execution further suggests that the drawing was done as an independent composition or as an advanced preparation for a painting. Related pictures are LV 8, 34, 56, 85, but none corresponds exactly. Compare for function with No. 23; for composition with No. 6.

The verso (Pl. 61), when the recto is turned upside down, shows a study in red chalk of the legs and a hand of a man. Two other such studies occur in this collection (versos 15, 29; Pl. 61). They seem to be typical academic works drawn from live models, and they were clearly cut off at half height, which indicates that they precede the respective rectos and that Claude no longer deemed them important in their own right. Apart from this album, at least four other academic studies in red chalk survive on the versos of elaborate drawings. Two of those are whole figures, not cut, on the back of early landscapes (D 21, 172). All the others are cut and occur on the back of drawings from ca. 1640 (D 485, 552), except for No. 29 here, whose recto belongs to the late forties. For lack of comparison, it is hard to date these nudes, but they seem compatible with Claude's manner of the thirties (compare Nos. 27–29). Sandrart, who knew the artist until 1635, explains that his figures "remain unpleasant in spite of the fact that he takes great pains and works hard on them and drew for many years in Rome in the academies from life and from statues." The extant nudes are thus only the smallest remainder of a once huge production.

W 49. D 464.

6 *Landscape Composition*

204 × 268 mm. Black chalk, pen, deep brown wash. Date: 1635–40.
The basic layout and the motifs of this drawing compare with the preceding sheet, but the more finished execution conveys the effect of an independent image. Firmer than the average nature drawing, it is on the other hand less complex than a painting; there are no figures, no details in the foreground, and the spatial expanse is limited. One may assume that the drawing was done in the studio. The composition is governed by a regular succession of planes from the dark foreground triangle on the left, to the brightly illuminated middle zone on the right, and to the distant hills. The left and right halves are contrasting (horizontal and open, vertical and closed), yet the entire image is also tightly framed by the dark foreground and the house on one hand, and by the clusters of trees on the other hand. Part of the secret of Claude's art is that his strong compositional patterns never become rigid. The execution is enlivened by the basic contrasts between the plain areas of deep wash, the altogether empty, illuminated portions, and the two grades of dense penwork in the foliage. While there are many related compositions in the years around 1640 (LV 41, 58), none is directly linked with this.

W 7. D 467.

7 *The Villa of Maecenas in Tivoli*

212 × 312 mm. Deep brown wash, black chalk, some pen strokes in the building. Inscribed on the verso in red chalk *CLAVO* and numbered in pen *Cl. 2* (not visible before the sheet was detached). Watermark: fleurs-de-lis in an oval. Date: ca. 1640.
The landscape around Tivoli appears as one of the artist's favorite sources of inspiration in numerous drawings (here Nos. 13, 26, 32) and several paintings. The building shown here and recurring in No. 26 is one of Tivoli's formerly famous Roman monuments, the so-called Villa of Maecenas below the park of Villa d'Este. It is nowadays disfigured by a paper factory. By the side is one of the smaller cascades. The drawing, probably done on the spot, is one of Claude's most brilliant nature views. It has a compelling pictorial unity, due both to the handling and the composition. In conformity with the inherent quality of the watercolor, the wash is applied in sweeping surfaces of

an almost abstract quality, accentuated by some finer strokes along the outline of the foreground. There are surprisingly few details, yet the illusion of reality is complete. The image consists of two planes separated by a diagonal and rendered in alternating zones of deep and light wash. The mass of the building and rocks is balanced by the trees silhouetted against the sky. A similar compositional scheme recurs in Nos. 11 and 16.

Claude's paraph on the back indicates that the sheet belonged to a now dispersed book of nature drawings of the same size numbered by him (mostly on the lower right of the recto) up to 70. Half of the sheets are known today, six being in this collection (Nos. 8–11, 13, 14). They formed an album—one of the twelve listed in Claude's inventory—which was in all likelihood an original sketchbook. The paper is mostly, but perhaps not always, the same except for the last sheets which are blue. None is dated, but circumstantial evidence points to the fact that all are from the years 1638–42. It cannot be proven that they were done in the order of their numbers, but it is probable. To the detailed enumeration given in D., page 62, the following numbers can now be added: D 443 (numbered *2*), 437 *(5)*, 431 *(9)*, 538 *(-8)*, 539 *(70)*.

W 57. D 512.

8 *The Cascades of Tivoli*

223 × 320 mm. Black chalk, light gray wash. Numbered in pen *10* on the upper left and illegibly at the right edge. Inscribed on the verso in red chalk, upside down, *CLAV.R.IV* (for Roma in urbe). From the same book as No. 7. Watermark: fleur-de-lis in an oval. Date: ca. 1640.

Nature is here again shaped into an even pattern of rocks and shrubbery rendered with regular hatchings and short strokes respectively. The view is symmetrical, the strongest contrasts of tone being in the foreground, which remains boldly open except for a dark diagonal edge of the nearest platform. The rocks on the left form an oblique mass, those on the right are built up as three horizontal platforms.

Continuing the style of late chalk drawings by Bril (see D 1198), Claude achieves a perfect balance between realism and simplification of form. This style recurs in a few other chalk drawings of rocks from those years (particularly D 437, 444, 470, coming from the same numbered sketchbook). The buildings above the three cascades on the right seem to be part of Tivoli,

with the temple of the Sibyl. Very much the same view as on this drawing, but completed by a framing tree, recurs in a painting by Jan Frans van Bloemen (G. Torselli, *La Galleria Doria*, Rome 1968, fig. 431).

W 41. D 438.

9 *View Outside Piazza del Popolo in Rome*

222 × 320 mm. Black chalk, gray wash, on the right a touch of brown wash. Pen frame. Numbered *17* at the lower right. Inscribed on the verso in red chalk *CLAVD.Ro IV*. From the same book as No. 7. Watermark: fleurs-de-lis in an oval. Date: ca. 1640.

Though the site has long since been altered and built over, the factual evidence and the comparison with drawings of the same spot by other artists of the time prove that Claude adhered exactly to what he saw. This includes the rising foreground. The church is Sta. Maria del Popolo; to the right is the obelisk of the square. The large Porta del Popolo is almost totally hidden by the trees. Yet the question of topography loses its importance in view of the fascinating and spirited page layout. As in No. 4, the forms are bound together into a compact surface which in this case ascends slightly in a rhythmical outline. Surface effect and grouping in depth match each other. The bulk of the trees and of the buildings occupies the center as two equal halves; the distance is given on the two narrower endings by the small shapes of the vertical trees. Despite its apparent casualness, the drawing has thus an inner coherence which explains why it does not affect us as a work left unfinished. Conversely, the empty areas of the paper read as sky and as solid foreground. The frame line and above all the oxen in their forceful repoussoir positioning enhance the pictorial unity of this singularly forward-looking nature drawing. Compare D 471.

W 52. D 448.

10 *Pastoral Landscape*

220 × 320 mm. Black chalk, brown wash for the lower part, light gray wash for the trees. Pen frame. Numbered *34* at the lower right. Inscribed on the verso in red chalk *CLAV Ro IV*. From the same book as No. 7. Date: ca. 1640.

Claude's innate sense for classical clarity is strongly felt in this admirable nature drawing. Horizontal matches vertical; the dark foreground matches the light background; the three groups of animals are symmetrically displayed. (There are even two pairs of small figures on opposite sides.) Equally evident is the separation of the technical means according to planes: Claude would begin with the chalk, using it in broad strokes for the foreground, in a soft, rounded manner for the trees, in more detailed, delicate strokes for the distance, which is almost absorbed by light. The two shades of the wash further clarify the spatial succession. All of this combines to suggest the atmosphere of a serene day full of light. The same valley, which may be in the Tiburtine hills, appears seen from a different angle in another drawing (D 475). While the logical distinction of technical media occurs not infrequently during the fifties (Nos. 32, 37), it is rarer at the time of this drawing; No. 14, coming from the same sketchbook, may be compared with it.

W 59. D 477.

11 Hilly Countryside

217 × 316 mm. Pen, shades of brown wash. The verso, now laid bare, is inscribed in red chalk *Clav Ro* and numbered in pen *36*. Watermark: fleur-de-lis in an oval. From the same book as No. 7. Date: ca. 1640.
The scenery is reminiscent of the countryside around Marino. (The white surface spared out in the distance might be Lake Albano.) The drawing makes a particularly majestic effect because of the imposing trees, the arid scenery of the distance, the strong spatial recession, and the loaded atmosphere. This has until now led to a later dating, supported by stylistic affinities with No. 32. It has now become obvious that this sheet too belongs to the time around 1640. It shows a pattern of contrasts in setting and technique similar to other nature views of the numbered album from which it comes (compare mainly Nos. 7 and 16, of 1639); bold trees placed against the light in the foreground, three horizontal, increasingly illuminated planes on the opposite side. The vigorous penwork and the play of bright sunlight and dark shadows in the trees compares with the Subiaco drawing of 1642 (D 483; cf. also D 482). The setting brings to mind the painting LV 39. Even the pen frame, drawn freehand, confirms in its energetic duct the proposed date. The heroic quality of the drawing, which anticipates the fifties,

gives a measure of Claude's artistic range at the peak of his exploration of nature.
The verso (Pl. 64, intensified), turned sideways, shows a faint outline sketch in black chalk of a steep gorge with a river, cascade, and double-arched bridge in the center. The closest parallels to this scenery are a few drawings of torrents and cascades from ca. 1640 (D 433–435, 444, 478).

W 56. D 708.

12 View of the Acqua Acetosa

220 × 323 mm. Pen, brown wash. Date: ca. 1640.
The Acqua Acetosa, a famous bend of the Tiber a mile or so upstream of Ponte Molle, used to be cherished for its charm and peacefulness. It was visited and drawn by many artists. Claude himself drew it at various times (D 591, 876), and the backgrounds of some of his early paintings give the feeling of being idealized records of the site (LV 42). This collection also contains (No. 46) a very different rendering of it from 1662. The present sheet is done with a remarkable economy of means. Large portions of the drawing remain white, yet read as foreground, river, and sky. The large tree and the shrub enclose the center of the view, which is accentuated by a few details, including the fountain, whereas the sides of the middle distance are kept in plain wash surfaces. An advanced date has so far been proposed for the drawing, but the redating of the preceding sheet and further parallels with nature drawings around 1640 point to a dating around 1640 or within the following few years. Compare D 288 for the shrubs, D 537 for the tree; even the duct of the pen frame confirms this dating. At the same time, the crisp style and the penwork anticipate nature drawings of the late forties (Nos. 26, 32).

W 44. D 875.

13 Wooded Landscape with Bridge

222 × 320 mm. Black chalk, pen, shades of brown wash. Numbered *50* at the lower right. Inscribed on the verso in red chalk *CLAV Ro*. Watermark: fleur-de-lis in an oval. From the same book as No. 7. Date: ca. 1640.

Rustic bridges of this type occur several times in Claude's drawings and paintings around 1640 (D 531, from the same numbered book, with a similar bridge below Tivoli; LV 60). This view, no doubt taken on the spot, forms an especially stately image. The lower part contains the bridge which actively spans the whole width, and the dark stripe at the bottom with the cattle in the center. The short, straight pen strokes and strong contrasts of tone of this portion are set against the upper part with its closing surface effect. Here, the regular pattern of the pen outlines for foliage and rocks and the even layers of wash again account for the stylistic unity of the sheet.

W 53. D 530.

14 A Sunlit Landscape with Trees

224 × 320 mm. On blue paper. Black chalk, brown wash for the bottom and the right, the rest in light gray-brown wash; pen frame and a few pen strokes at the upper right. Numbered 70 at the bottom right of the verso. Date: ca. 1640.

The newly appeared number on the reverse designates the drawing as coming from the numbered book (see No. 7), the last few pages of which are of blue paper. (Whether D 843 indeed belonged to the book too may be open to question.) More perfunctory than the otherwise comparable nature view No. 10, this sheet astonishes for its impressionistic qualities. The image is created with the minimum of forms and means that often characterizes Claude's studies from nature of this time. The wash zones and the tree branch on the top enclose the central group of trees, which is flanked on either side by more distant hills. While the middle ground is taken together as a shaded zone, the foreground shows the contrast of dark wash and white surfaces which are spared out, yet act as illuminated terrain. Corot and Cézanne are prophetically anticipated. The blue paper, which Claude used for half of the *Liber Veritatis* drawings and for a number of others, mostly among his finest works (here No. 37), provides an additional dimension of tone.

W 42. D 539.

15 View of the Tiber Valley

228 × 325 mm. The foreground is in brown wash, the distance in a light gray-brown tone. Date: ca. 1640.

The site represented here was among Claude's favorite sketching grounds, about five miles upstream of Ponte Molle. The same area, seen from different viewpoints, occurs in other nature drawings (D 277, 424) and re-appears, idealized, in the backgrounds of some paintings. It is readily seen that the drawing ranks among the finest in this most difficult of techniques, the pure wash (compare No. 2). Throughout, one can follow Claude's brilliant manipulation of the brush in large areas, some with a crisp edge, in dots and fine lines, charged or thinned out, dry or—as in the shrubs on the left—blended together while still wet. The daring absence of tall motifs insures a spacious feeling and a modern look. Under the apparent casualness of the image lies a conscious structure: foreground and distance are strongly contrasted in scale, tone, and shape; the central protuberance, echoed by the distant tower and the flanking shrubs given with a minimum of detail, are the three main accents of the view. The middle ground consists of dots which enliven the spared out areas; the distance is taken together as a light wash surface. The style conforms to the nature drawings of about 1640.

The verso (Pl. 61) shows a study in red chalk of a man carrying a bag on his shoulders; it is cut off at the bottom. Almost certainly done from a live model, this is the most elaborate of Claude's few nudes; see catalog entry No. 5. One is reminded of the tiny figures carrying bales of goods which occur in nearly every one of his seaport paintings up to ca. 1640.

W 51. D 425.

16 Pastoral Landscape

232 × 333 mm. Black chalk, brown wash, pen at the bottom and for the frame, touches of heightening at the upper left. Inscribed on the verso *Claud IV/fecit 1639;* the outlines of the middle distance are traced through in black chalk.

The compositional scheme of this brilliant wash drawing, consisting of two contrasting planes, is basically that found in Nos. 7 and 11. The dark foreground with its rich silhouette of leaves, flocks, and a shepherd outlined against the light provides a pictorial frame for the compact middle ground with its more minute internal design. The bottom zone lets the almost empty intermediary area of the river and the opposite bank appear as drenched in sunlight. The trees bring to mind those in No. 7. More pictorially worked out than most nature drawings, this sheet shows a particularly tight layout, has a figure scene, a high degree of finish, and a signature, all of which point to its being an independent image. Whether it was done out of doors or in the studio is hard to say and does not greatly matter. On the other hand, the composition is considerably less complex than that of a painting. The newly appeared date is all the more important as only three more dated nature drawings from the thirties are known. It calls for some readjustment of a few proposed dates, and it cautions us to avoid pressing for too precise datings; thus, it may not seem "logical" that this sheet should precede by three years the Subiaco study of 1642 (D 483).

W 46. D 624.

17 *Wooded Landscape*

207 × 283 mm. Paper tinted reddish on the recto. Black chalk, brown wash. Signed at the bottom *CLAVDIO f.* Date: 1640–50.
This plein-air view in the Campagna again reveals Claude's masterful skill in the pure wash technique. Seemingly casual, the view is in fact carefully arranged. The bottom zone consists of plain layers of wash in two shades. Trees and a large, horizontal branch enclose the distant view which is dominated by the outline of a palace (compare D 403). This inner view is set off from the foreground by a zone of white—a device found not infrequently in Claude's nature drawings (D 387). Moreover, the two halves of the drawing can be read as contrasting, almost independent scenes, the left being an open view, the right a wooded area with two nearly imperceptible figures resting in the dark zone at the edge of the road (for the right side, compare the right halves of D 420, 472, 544). At the same time, a regular pattern of the brushwork in plain, large areas or in short, dry touches accounts for the unity of the whole drawing. Stylistic parallels are the drawings D 676–678, which would point to a date in the later forties. On the verso (Pl. 63), the main forms of the trees are traced through in black chalk, the outlines of the distance in pen. The two media emphasize the

spatial effect. Similar tracings occur on quite a few of Claude's drawings (D 307 v, 422 v, 482 v); the brittle duct of the pen results from holding the sheet against the window.

W 38. D 551.

18 *A Group of Pastoral Figures*

192 × 260 mm. Pen, brown wash, light wash for the sky. Date: 1640–45. Probably the earliest of the fifteen elaborate figure drawings of the album, this is also the earliest such example to be carried out as a finished, autonomous work. Like some other drawings of this type, it was presumably done in connection with the figures of a painting, then completed into a forceful image by the addition of a surrounding. The nearest parallel to the figures is in the painting LV 56 (1641), where the two standing women occur similarly (on the canvas, they are an inch smaller). The figures seem at first sight to illustrate a specific story, but the occurrence of similar, yet somewhat different groups in several other works makes it clear that they must be regarded as merely pastoral. At this stage Claude has already abandoned the bambocesque genre scenes of his early years (D 186, 329) in favor of a Raphaelesque classicism, but the bucolic spirit of this work still precedes the heroic style of his later figures. Compare the two women with the late No. 52 (after Raphael).

W 27. D 461. Roethlisberger, *op. cit. sub* No. 1, p. 50.

19 *Seaport*

188 × 265 mm. Pen. Traced through on the verso (Pl. 63), both sides piercing through. Date: ca. 1640.
Based on Bril and Tassi, Claude's imaginary antique seaports, or "perspectives," as his biographer Baldinucci calls them, made the fame of the young artist. They culminate in two dozen examples painted from 1635 to 1645, whereas few date from later. Claude must have prepared their complicated designs in many studies, of which only a handful survive, this one

being the most revealing. Together with three other studies for the same composition (D 455 ff.), it gives us an insight into the searching creative process for what was to become Claude's finest seaport to that date, the *Embarkation of St. Ursula* (LV 54; 1641). The drawing represents an early *pensée* which Claude was still to modify thoroughly; some of its motifs recur in the two subsequent paintings of seaports (LV 63, 80). In all likelihood the present recto was the first to be drawn, and the other side was the tracing. The verso is both clearer and more summary and shows throughout minor differences (balustrade in front, large palace façade, view across the portico, distant temple). The main diagonals of the recto and the additional grid lines of the verso are a device frequently found in Claude's compositional drawings (see Nos. 21, 49); here, they can only have served as a generic check of compositional equilibrium.

W 30. D 454.

20 Landscape Composition

217 × 317 mm. Black chalk, pen, gray wash, slight brown wash in the foreground. Date: ca. 1640.
The function of this drawing is similar to that of the preceding seaport: it is a searching compositional study for a painting, certainly done in the studio. It still differs in every portion from the final work, which belongs to Claude's important paintings and dates from 1640/41 (LV 53; owned by the Duke of Bedford). Among the class of compositional drawings, which increases in number with Claude's years, this sheet is easily the finest known example up to its date. When it is compared with drawings from nature, one notices a greater complexity in the development of the space from the foreground over many successive levels to the remote distance—complexity which results from the dimensions of the planned painting. What mattered to the artist at this point was the manipulation of the scenic elements; typically, the details of figures and buildings are still missing. The animated handling conveys a sense of immediacy, and the use of two tones of wash enhances the pictorial effect.
The verso (Pl. 62, intensified), when the recto is turned upside down, shows a faint sketch in black chalk of three figures in a landscape surrounding with rocks on the left. They resemble the only other extant study of the painting LV 53 (D 401), but differ from the rural dance on the painting itself. The

figure on the right is female and classical; the group brings to mind the subject of Diana, Cephalus, and Procris. Compare D 703 v.

W 58. D 400.

21 Landscape with Rural Dance

263 × 193 mm. Black chalk, pen, brown wash. Horizon and squaring with diagonals in black chalk. Signed at the bottom left *Claudio Gillee*. Ten inch marks by Claude along the right border (cf. No. 41). The verso is numbered *3* at the bottom and inscribed in pen *Claudio Gille,* then covered up by wash is: ... *al* (?) *15 Gio. Batt. Remigi* (unknown). Watermark: cross flanked by P, F, in an oval. Date: 1642.
In 1642 Claude repeated on a small scale his then largest classical seaport, done a couple of years earlier for the King of Spain. He created as a pendant, *ex novo* a pastoral landscape with flocks driven over a bridge (LV 62). This drawing is a first and subsequently modified *pensée* for this painting. The penwork, which compares with the preceding sheet, shows a fascinating array of graphic idiosyncrasies according to the kind of foliage or object it describes. The country dance with numerous figures is a theme found throughout Claude's maturity (cf. No. 29), three times coupled with a seaport pendant. Here, the complex layout suggests a painting of larger size than the one executed in the end. The squaring is again Claude's simple house rule for ascertaining the compositional balance (and not, as Kitson would have it, a means of transfer onto the canvas); its practical use can easily be verified by the viewer.
The verso (Pl. 64, intensified) shows on the left half a faint, experimental sketch in black chalk for the setting of the seaport pendant (LV 61): a framing portico with horizontal steps, a boat in the foreground as in the painting, but larger, and the distant frontal palace moved to the left.

W 34. D 496.

22 Classical Landscape

206 × 292 mm. Paper tinted brown (or brown paper?). Black chalk, brown wash, white heightening. The frame line cut on two sides. Watermark: bird on three mounts in a circle. Date: 1640–45.

This independent composition is unusual in color and layout. If the use of the tinted ground is in itself not rare, the brown tone is, and the pictorial combination with a shining sky recurs only once (D 704). The inner proportions, comprising a spatial development over many steps, are those of a painting. The constructive firmness, resulting from the emphasis on verticals and horizontals and such motifs as the edifices on the right and the waterfall, brings to mind the art of Domenichino toward whose compositions Claude became increasingly receptive during the forties. This is most evident in Claude's pastorals of the time, which in fact have many similarities with this sheet (LV 95, 102, 103). For the precise handling, compare chalk drawings of ca. 1640 (D 453, 304).

W 6. D 557.

23 Study for a Pastoral Landscape

211 × 312 mm. Black chalk, light gray wash. Watermark: bird on three mounts in a circle. Date: ca. 1644.

Because of the soft chalk technique and the summary design of the foreground, this work at first brings to mind the nature drawings of the time (Nos. 8, 10, 14). But the setting as a whole and motifs such as the tower soon make it clear that it is a first *pensée* for a painting, done in the studio (although Claude would normally prefer the pen for this purpose). The open foreground, as in No. 20, and the sweeping execution assign it to a more experimental level than the chalk composition No. 5. It represents the starting point for the painting LV 83, now in the British royal collection, and for the subsequent studies preparing LV 90 (D 578); also LV 85 shows affinities with it. In the foreground the three pictures have a pastoral scene. The unity and the particular beauty of this drawing reside in the generous freedom of its handling. Passages like the left side anticipate Cézanne's draftsmanship.

W 48. D 561.

24 Judgment of Paris

182 × 261 mm. Pen, dark brown wash. The drawing has now been backed and the holes which the ink had bitten into the paper filled. Date: ca. 1645.

Paris is brooding over his choice (compare No. 18); on the right are his dog, Minerva, Juno with the peacock, the crouching Venus with Amor at her feet, and Mercury taking off. This is Claude's most vigorous figure drawing, and in it the lesson of Carracci, the classical tradition, and the Roman high baroque all make themselves felt. It was executed as a preparatory work for the painting of 1644/45 (LV 94) in Washington. Claude had already treated the subject in a painting of 1633 and in a small drawing (D 371) from a series of the story of Paris, which comes closer to the painting of 1645. Until this time Claude had apart from this done very few mythological figures. The stocky and somewhat pedestrian types of this sheet still betray his earlier predilection for rural genre figures. In the painting the four figures are, as a result of a few changes, much more effectively grouped, and except for Juno they are appropriately given as elegant nudes.

W 25. D 597. Roethlisberger, *op. cit. sub* No. 1, pp. 44–54.

25 Hilly Landscape

179 × 253 mm. Pen, a touch of brown wash in the center, some accidental spots of dark wash. Inscribed on the verso *Claudio Gelle/fecit,* followed by *foequato.* The pen shows through. Date: ca. 1645.

The entire landscape and the absence of repoussoirs or other stage devices indicate that this drawing was done from nature. The crisp penmanship ultimately goes back to Titian's and Carracci's landscape drawings and has its parallel in Domenichino and Grimaldi. Comparison with the *Liber Veritatis* and other drawings places this work into the mid-forties. One may regret that Claude should have abandoned the virtuosity of his wash drawings from nature of the years around 1640. Henceforth, nature drawings become few and individual in type (here Nos. 26, 32, 46). To do justice to this drawing one must be aware of the purity of its means and of the admirable precision in the objective, topographical rendering. The planes are clearly separated into an empty foreground zone bordered by shrubs, a middle ground with trees, a cascade, and distant hills.

The verso (Pl. 63) shows two geometric pen sketches of a kind unique in Claude. Their purpose is unclear. Are they connected with his science of perspective? Does "foequato" allude to an equation?

W 4. D 574.

26 *Panorama from Tivoli*

209 × 314 mm. Pen, light brown wash. Two accidental spots show through from the verso. Inscribed on the verso *veduta di tivoli/claud/1647*.
The view is taken from the hills opposite Tivoli, towards the plain. The Villa of Maecenas on the left already appears in No. 7. The ease of the handling, the lightness of tone, and the technical restraint make this drawing a masterpiece *sui generis,* far from the grand style of the earlier wash drawings. Its form is deceptively simple. Above an empty bottom zone with some perspective lines, follow the area of the trees with its large hatchings, then successive planes in outline. The image is almost imperceptibly framed by the base plane, the building on the left, and the slightly taller tree on the extreme right, while a few distant trees attract the attention to the center. The whole is of utmost delicacy. Although Claude never made direct use of his nature drawings in painting, an echo of them may often be sensed in his pictures; thus, the distance of the pastoral landscape now in New York (LV 109) and dating from the same year, can be seen in conjunction with this drawing.
The verso (Pl. 62) shows a light, panoramic outline sketch in black chalk, no doubt taken from the surroundings of Tivoli. Its "minimal" approach is prophetic of Corot. Only the verso sketch of No. 34 (also Pl. 62) compares closely; see also the view from Tivoli No. 32. This is the kind of faint chalk sketch which underlies most drawings by Claude.

W 40. D 621.

27 *Study of Cattle*

170 × 237 mm. Red chalk, red wash, brown wash in the center. Paper affected by foxing. Date: 1640–50.
Cows were at all times Claude's favorite animal occurring often together with goats and sheep in almost every one of his landscape paintings. As for the trees, he needed many studies of them as *aide-mémoire* without copying them directly in the paintings. Of the seventy or so animal studies, most having belonged to a small album (D 199–267), this is the finest and largest; only one other is in sanguine. Compared with the other animal studies, the four oxen are pictorially grouped and more thoroughly rendered in their plasticity; see here the oxen in No. 9. It is hard to assign a precise date to these studies, but this one, in terms of the malleability of its form, is more advanced than the bulk of the animal album and has its closest parallels in drawings of the late forties (No. 29 and D 656).
The verso (Pl. 61), done in red chalk with a trifle of black chalk, shows a seated cat with a ribbon, a crouching cat, and two geometric sketches, perhaps for carpentry. The verso, which is cut on the right, must precede the uncut recto.

W 31. D 447.

28 *Rebekah at the Well*

186 × 247 mm. Black chalk. Ruled pen frame. Watermark: star in a circle. Date: 1645–50.
The exceptional character of this drawing lies in the light and easy handling of the chalk which evenly fills the surface. It anticipates French sanguines of the eighteenth century (Watteau, Natoire). Despite its lightness, the image is carefully framed in itself by the camels, the small fountain, the distant town gate on the left, and by further verticals and horizontals. The two figures and the camels are contrasted in frontal and profile position. The disposition of the figures echoes comparable groups of Rebekah and of Christ at the well by Poussin and Carracci. The theme of Rebekah and Eliezer (who more correctly should be an old man) does not recur elsewhere in Claude, but it fits well into the late forties when earlier pastoral subjects became charged with a new religious or mythological meaning, such as the country dance turned into the marriage of Rebekah (LV 113; 1648) or into a bacchanal (LV 108, painting recently rediscovered). A comparison with the figure groups of LV 113 reveals a similar mood in both. Although a later dating has been proposed for this sheet, the handling and the whole character of the scene now appear to belong to the late forties when figure drawings

appear more frequently than at other times. The chalk technique has its nearest parallel in the following sheet and in D 652, 656.

W 50. D 751.

29 *Rural Dance*

164 × 222 mm. Black chalk, brown wash for the lower section, gray wash above, a touch of red chalk. Date: 1645–50.

From the years around 1650 date a whole group of chalk drawings of figures done in preparation for specific paintings (D 608, 612, 656, 687, 692, 694). The present sheet belongs stylistically to this group of which it is the finest example. Similarly composed from imagination, it is more carefully worked out than the others and is made into a self-contained, framed image. The style is characterized by a broad, even handling of the chalk and by a reduction of the forms into large, plain areas. The juxtaposition of animals in two planes indicates depth and also accentuates the surface unity. The closest stylistic and thematic analogy is the drawing of a dance in the Louvre (D 652). The theme is found throughout Claude's maturity (see No. 21). In subject and spirit this sheet relates to the painting of the marriage of Rebekah (LV 113; 1648), which holds a key position in Claude's œuvre in regard to the treatment of the figures. Not a preliminary study, the drawing is an independent by-product.

The verso (Pl. 61), when the recto is turned upside down, shows a study in red chalk of the legs of a walking man, drawn from life. It was cut off at the top. See catalog entry No. 5 for a discussion.

W 16. D 651.

30 *Study of a Tree*

160 × 217 mm. Both faces are in pen over a black chalk underdrawing and have their frame partly cut off. Date: ca. 1650.

This drawing is of the upper portion of what appears to be a Roman pine tree. The same remarks made about No. 25 also apply to this study when it is compared with the tree drawing of 1633 (No. 3); the brilliance of a naturalistic rendering has here given way to restraint and objectivity, with a

beauty of its own. An intense animation and a more solid grasp of reality result from the crisp and incisive penwork with its interplay of hatchings and curls. Surface unity and the sensation of plasticity are present to an equal degree. The drawing in all probability was done from nature, but, as in the case of other nature studies dating after the forties, the type of image remains unique. The penwork compares with D 620v and 684 (*Liber* drawing 119). One is reminded of this sheet when looking at the trees in many paintings, although Claude never slavishly transposed such studies onto a canvas. His changed concept of reality accounts for the increasing number of pure pen drawings in the mature phase (cf. Nos. 25, 45, 53). On the verso (Pl. 63) the design is traced through but carried out to a lesser degree of finish. Compare D 537v, 575v, and others. The *raison d'être* for such reversals is hard to know. Presumably Claude was interested in testing the reversed effect or in clarifying the structure of foliage and branches. Or was he trying to draw left-handedly, as the hatchings might indicate here?

W 15. D 788.

31 *Landscape with Citadel*

177 × 249 mm. Black chalk, light brownish wash, pen frame. The upper left of the verso (not reproduced) contains a slight sketch of a figure in black chalk. Watermark: fleur-de-lis.

In the 1650s, the decade of Claude's most heroic paintings, there are a number of drawings which stand halfway between nature study and composition. This work and No. 34 are such examples. If Claude did the present sheet out-of-doors, he monumentalized the motifs and enhanced them by a symmetrical framework. Even so this view does not make a complete landscape composition for a painting; it has neither the spatial complexity nor the detailed foreground. As it stands the setting evokes first of all the famous breakthrough into classical landscape of the beginning of the century: Carracci's Aldobrandini lunette with the *Flight into Egypt*. (Compare No. 22 for another example of the impact exercised by the Bolognese on the mature Claude.) The dating of chalk drawings proves particularly difficult, for they may at various moments show an elusive consistency (as D 181v from the thirties; 683a and 703 from ca. 1650; 913 and 929 from the early sixties). The most likely date seems here to be the early fifties, at which time hill towns flanked by rocks and trees are especially numerous in paintings (LV 125, 128, 135). It is also true that the citadel is taken over identically in a pictorial sheet of the early sixties (D 880); the latter date cannot altogether be ruled out for this sheet.

W 24. D 702.

32   *View from Tivoli*

200 × 267 mm. Black chalk for the upper part, pen for the lower part and the frame line, two shades of brown wash. Inscribed at the bottom left of the verso *faict Claud 1651 tivoli*. Watermark: bird on three mounts in a circle. The view is taken from Tivoli northwards; the white area on the left must be haze (not a lake). Five successive parallel planes create one of the most stunning panoramic views. The foreground, with its liveried huntsmen boldly silhouetted against the light and with its contrasting dark and white stripes of ground, is followed by a hillside with tiny trees drawn in pen, then by a more distant, paler hill, and finally by a dark mountain and a mountain range created by a mere outline. The underlying structure is one of horizontals alternating with slight diagonals. The outlines of the huntsmen blend into the light wash laid over the whole area, resulting in an optical blur. Among the decreasing number of nature drawings, this is the last, or one of the last, done in Tivoli, the region that ten years earlier inspired so many drawings. Compared with them, this unique work has a deeper atmospheric content and a more condensed, though outwardly less dramatic energy (see also No. 26). A comparison with No. 11 offers a revealing insight into the consistency and the evolution of Claude's art.

W 5. D 707.

33   *Wooded Landscape*

194 × 280 mm. Paper tinted reddish. Black chalk, brown wash, white heightening, pen for the figure and the frame. Date: 1650–55.
About a dozen drawings by Claude with an attractive reddish ground are known (here also Nos. 17, 35), most belonging to his mature years. Tinted ground always accounts for a special, pictorial effect. This sheet combines the intimacy of a pastoral with the grandeur of a classical work. Its stylistic unity results from the simple layout in two parallel planes. The darker foreground contains large plants and, in the center, a sylvan god whose crowned head is the only form reaching into the bent, empty stripe separating the two planes. His presence crystallizes the contemplative mood of the drawing. The area at the bottom left corner brings into balance the opening on the right. In the trees the soft shades of wash combined with broad chalk create an admirably impressionistic effect (compare D 699, 950). Equally remote from nature studies and painted compositions, this is an independent and intensely poetic image. The dating is difficult. A date in the early sixties has been suggested, but I now see the drawing more in conjunction with the heroic years of the fifties.
The verso (not reproduced) contains, along the top and bottom, three faint sketches in black chalk of wide steps and an extended balustrade done in connection with an architectural scene such as LV 120, 132 (not identical); compare D 679v.

W 9. D 877.

34   *Heroic Landscape*

260 × 398 mm. Black chalk, light gray-brown wash, the bottom and the extreme right also in pen and brown wash, the distance in light bluish wash. Date: ca. 1650–52.
The splendor of this large drawing, one of Claude's masterpieces, speaks for itself. The scenery and the trees suggest that it was done, or at least begun, out of doors, which is confirmed by the verso sketch. At the same time nature is, by simplification and augmentation, elevated into the realm of heroic grandeur. The palm tree and the narrow bottom zone form the pictorial frame for the majestic group of trees—a stately central tree flanked by lighter ones of other species. The castle is enclosed by the foreground stage and the wood. The light wash adds tone and color and binds the whole surface together. The increase in Claude's range of expression can be measured if this work is compared with his earlier nature drawings done largely in the same technique of broad chalk (Nos. 8, 10). For the date, all indications point to the early fifties. The setting is the graphic equivalent to the paintings LV 119 and 125. See also the drawings D 635, 697–706.

The verso (Pl. 62), done in black chalk, shows an outline sketch of a view over a valley with trees and a castle near the foreground.

W 35. D 709.

35 *Journey to Emmaus*

172 × 226 mm. Paper tinted reddish (see No. 33). Black chalk, deep brown wash for the trees and the bottom, pink body color and much white heightening (partly flaked off) for the figures. Date: 1652.

Judging from the drawing in the *Liber Veritatis* (LV 125), the lost painting of the *Journey to Emmaus* from 1652 must have been an especially important and fairly large work of Claude from the beginning of his heroic phase. The figures of this drawing correspond to those of the painting. Another less finished and still different study for the three figures, drawn on both faces, survives (D 710). The present sheet evokes what must have been a spectacular sunset atmosphere with the light falling from behind. These powerful figures have a nobility of their own. In the painting the awkward hardness of Christ's arm was surely smoothed out. Like some other figure drawings, this work must have been done as a final detail preparation when the landscape on the canvas was nearing completion and Claude came—at last, as always—to the figures. Simultaneously, he made the drawing into an autonomous image by adding the surrounding landscape elements, which take up the tree motifs of the painting but are adapted in scale to the drawing.

W 13. D 711.

36 *View of S. Agnese Fuori le Mura*

149 × 207 mm. Pen for the foreground, black chalk for the distance, brown wash. Date: 1650–55.

Despite its venerable age, this church in the outskirts of Rome, on Via Nomentana, has rarely been illustrated by artists. The view is taken from the bottom of the hill, towards the façade, with the circular Sta. Costanza appearing immediately to the right, somewhat too close to S. Agnese. Seen from closer by, the church also appears in another drawing by Claude from the same time (D 723). More than in his earlier nature studies, the unas-

suming immediacy of this sheet captures the poetic charm of the spot. Even today, a sense of seclusion emerges from the site, although the church is now surrounded by modern buildings blocking the view of the distant Alban hills, which Claude has increased in size. The open foreground and left side, both rounded off, contribute to the vignette-like character of the image. However, the contrasts are also clearly set between the dark figures (which may remind one of Rembrandt etchings), the dark foliage on the right, and the bright zones next to them. In date, the drawing cannot be far from the view of Tivoli of 1651 (No. 32).

W 32. D 724.

37 *Apollo as Herdsman and Mercury*

194 × 271 mm. On blue paper. Gray wash, pen for the bottom and the frame line, brown wash in the lower part, white heightening. Date: 1654.

Apollo, as herdsman of Admetus, is piping while the herds are being stolen by Mercury. This cheerful, Ovidian story combines Claude's early predilection for the pastoral genre (see the treatment of Apollo) with his later interest in the classical world. From the mid-forties onward he represented the various episodes of the story in no fewer than eight paintings and in quite a few drawings. The dominant note of this sheet is its tonal color—a personal achievement of Claude, even if one is reminded of chiaroscuro woodcuts and certain Neapolitan drawings of the time. The effect is characterized by the economy of design and media as well as by the contrast of tone and scale from the bottom zone to the two increasingly diaphanous planes above. The drawing relates to the painting LV 128, of 1654, destroyed by fire in 1870; Apollo and the herds are the same as in the *Liber* record after the painting, Mercury differs slightly, and the surrounding scenery is abbreviated. As in the case of other figure drawings, which are most numerous in the decade of the 1650s, it was probably done as an ultimate model for the figure details of the picture, but completed into an autonomous image. The theme recurs six years later in No. 44, and the very same type of drawing as this is found twenty-five years later (D 1016).

On the verso (not reproduced) are sketches in black chalk with some white of three seated goats (cf. D 145v, 255, 535v).

W 19. D 721.

38 *Heroic Landscape*

222 × 330 mm. Pen, deep brown wash, also gray wash for the middle distance, white heightening in the foreground. Date: 1655–58.
While most of Claude's elaborate compositional drawings are either advanced preparations for a specific painting or final, autonomous works, this splendid sheet is unusual for its particularly searching character. The foreground, comprising the framing tree, the platform, and the figures, is treated most intensely. The distance is enclosed by the trees and the threatening clouds. The left side is less firmly shaped. The drawing is an experimental *pensée* for a large painting in the mood of the monumental biblical works of the fifties, which form the peak of Claude's maturity. The figures ascending a hill—a motif going back to Carracci—are not a fully defined subject. The composition must represent the first stage for the painting of David (LV 145; 1658; see also the following number): not only does the setting qualify as a scene for this subject, but the basic disposition of the forms is already that of the final work, and the two men occur likewise in a further preliminary drawing (D 809) where there are, as here, no other figures. The man on the left even seems to be carrying the crucial helmet full of water. The absence of the principal figures of David and his suite would be in line with many other first studies (cf. No. 20), all the more so as this complicated group would have required a special study.
The verso (not reproduced) contains various pen sketches: clouds similar to those of the recto, two men, and four sketches for a cassone the inner panels of which are decorated with a sunrise over a coast view.

W 60, 61. D 771 (the verso reproduced both times).

39 *David and the Three Heroes*

259 × 362 mm. Pen, yellow-brown and brown wash, white heightening. Inscribed at the bottom *disigne faict del quadro de principe Don Agustino/ Claudio G./I.V.F. Roma* and, below David, *Davide al desert*. Watermark: bird on three mounts in a circle. Date: 1658.
This most sumptuous among Claude's figure drawings corresponds to the figure portion of his large painting in which King David stoically refuses to accept a drink of water fetched for him by three heroes in the enemy camp (LV 145; 1658). The figures here are exactly those of the painting, where they are twice as large. The surrounding rocks and trees, too, are based on the painted ones, but are somewhat altered in the interest of forming a complete image. The style of the figures, strongly influenced by late antique reliefs, and the motif of the rocks, are in keeping with the grave subject. "Faict del quadro" indicates that the drawing repeats, rather than prepares, the essential portion of the picture. The *raison d'être* of this sheet, as confirmed by the inscription and by analogous papal works of Claude, is the prestigious patron, Prince Agostino Chigi, the twenty-three year old nephew of the reigning pope. The choice of the subject directly alludes to the probity governing the conduct of the young prince in his powerful position. Thematically related is the drawing of Artaxerxes (D 812) which formerly belonged to this album.

W 55. D 810.

40 *Assault of a Citadel*

228 × 331 mm. Black chalk, pen for the foreground, yellow-brown and brown wash, white and yellow heightening. Date: ca. 1658.
In many ways this altogether extraordinary drawing recalls the preceding sheet with the story of David. But it has a more searching quality and does not relate to a painting. Only in the fifties would Claude conceive so heroic and dramatic an image. The theme of the battle, essentially foreign to Claude's art, occurs only in the combat on the bridge (LV 137), done for Alexander VII Chigi. The drawing is clearly organized. The antique warriors, who all seem to belong to the same party, push across the lower half in a consciously rhythmical symmetry (and not in a baroque mêlée). Two tree trunks with a narrow platform halt the movement on the right. The left half opens on a distant view; the contrasting right half is filled by trees and a citadel overlooking the lake. In the foreground the firm handwriting of the pen in short, often parallel strokes produces an admirable graphic pattern the unity of which is echoed in the background by the more muted register of the chalk. The setting and the pictorial execution, which owes much to the use of a colored ground and white body-color, conveys to the drawing the quality of an independent work. For a study of a painting the composition would have to be more complex. Nevertheless, the similarity to the David

drawing suggests that Claude was thinking in terms of a painting, of which this would be the central portion, perhaps of a battle of David or another Old Testament battle as a pendant to the extant picture. The medieval citadel would not be suitable for a Roman battle.

W 47. D 813.

41 *Esther on Her Way to Ahasuerus*

190 × 258 mm. Black chalk, pen, brown wash, white heightening at the bottom. The lower margin is divided into inches. Date: 1657–59.
The painting of Esther, done in 1659 for the Bishop of Montpellier, was Claude's largest and, according to his own words, also his most beautiful work (LV 146). Only the left third of it survives, and that in poor condition. This sheet is a first and subsequently modified *pensée* for the painting. Esther appears under the trees; a messenger is receiving her in front of the palace. Babylon is imagined as a classical Roman city with a Pantheon-like structure on the right. The spatial complexity of the image, which contains a wealth of palaces, figures, and trees, and extends over many planes, is indicative of a very large painting. Not as detailed as most of Claude's preparatory studies, the drawing is above all a study in the basic disposition of masses, forms, and light. This is achieved by an exceptional vigor in the handling of the pen and the brush. As a rule in such studies the details are given larger than they would appear on the canvas. In spite of the bold execution, the setting is organized symmetrically with two contrasting halves; the orthogonal structure is basically similar to the preceding sheet. The composition is lastly based on the *Procession of Delphi* (LV 119) and on the *Landing of Cleopatra* (LV 63) and anticipates in turn the *Oracle of Delphi* (LV 157) and the *View of Delos* (LV 179). A second preliminary drawing for Esther in the British Museum (D 817) is more neatly worked out, even more heroic in the display of the motifs, and comes much closer to the final work; the trees now take the place of the palace on the left. See the following sheet for the figures.

W 14. D 816.

42 *Esther on Her Way to Ahasuerus*

189 × 247 mm. Pen, brown wash, white heightening. The left margin is inscribed *palma 4'*; at the bottom one makes out under the heightening *tela imperatore palma 6* and *ESTER*. The entire width is marked off into six sections along the bottom; four such sections are indicated on the vertical line in the center. The verso is signed in the center *Claudio Gillee/inventore fecit/Roma 1659*.
This forceful figure drawing is a final model for the main group of the painting, the whole composition of which is prepared in the preceding sheet. The details still differ from the final version in which there are only a herald and two dogs. In accordance with the scale of the drawing, the surrounding scenery is kept narrow so as to form at the same time a complete image (compare similarly Nos. 35, 39, and other figure studies). The generous use of heightening results in a pictorial style which is very Roman and has its parallel in drawings by Pietro da Cortona. The "imperial size" refers to the area the figures were to occupy on the canvas; the vertical line coincides with the middle of the picture. The scaling along the edge occurs in a few other drawings by Claude (here Nos. 21, 41, 51).

W 11. D 818.

43 *Landscape with the Flight into Egypt*

187 × 255 mm., the corners cut. Pen, light brown wash, a touch of heightening for the Virgin. Inscribed in the center of the verso *Claudio Gelle/1660 Roma*.
In conformity with the subject of the Flight into Egypt, which was at all times one of Claude's favorites, the character of this drawing is gentle and pleasing. It makes a complete composition, perhaps done as an end in itself. The handling is both controlled and rich; the regular penwork in short, broad strokes and the generous wash produce an especially pictorial effect. The view consists of only two planes, with the distant lake matching the pyramid on the right. The horizon is at half height; the three main trees form a square measuring half the width of the image. The intimacy of the design does not relate to any other work of the time but brings to mind two

small paintings on copper from the mid-forties (cf. the catalog of the paintings, figures 160, 194).

W 3. D 748.

44 Apollo as Herdsman and Mercury

148 × 204 mm. Paper tinted yellowish brown. Pen and gray ink, gray wash.
Date: ca. 1660.

The subject and the function of the drawing are the same as in No. 37, but the effect changes greatly on account of color and technique. The two planes are not differentiated in the handling. The disposition of the foreground resembles the figure portion in the painting LV 152 (1660/61). Also Mercury driving away the cattle occurs similarly, but smaller, in the painting. The drawing must thus relate to the picture in much the same way as the other example, viz. as a final model for the figures which was made at the same time into a little image in its own right. The difference is that in this instance the details correspond less closely; the painting shows goats, not sheep.

W 18. D 850.

45 Coast Scene

165 × 227 mm. A touch of brown wash at the bottom and on the left.
Inscribed in the center of the verso *A Roma ce 8 mars 1662.*

After 1650 the busy seaports (cf. No. 19) which had brought Claude great fame ceased completely. They were followed by a small number of lonely coast landscapes. This drawing stands, thus, somewhat isolated in its time. No longer a pure seaport in the former sense, its type may be compared with LV 120 and 132. The temple with the statue of Fortune—perhaps an evocation of the antique Anzio—recurs in the same years in LV 157 and 164. The composition does not relate directly to any other work, and the relatively simple scenery would not be suitable for a projected painting. The pure pen-work is particularly frequent in the sixties (see No. 53). In technique and setting, this sheet may be seen as a by-product of Claude's renewed interest

in etching, which led him in the sixties to publish seven etchings, including a reproduction of the seaport with St. Ursula (D 944).

W 23. D 865.

46 View of the Acqua Acetosa

220 × 317 mm. Black chalk, light gray-brown wash, pen frame. Inscribed at the bottom *Claudio fecit/Roma 1662 le dernier/ iour de l'ané iour de St. Silvestre alla acetosa.*

The place is the same as that of No. 12 made twenty years earlier. Done on the last day of the year, the drawing, because of its gray tone, evokes a winter day even though the trees have much foliage. This is one of the few elaborate nature views from Claude's late years. The uniform, restrained execution in calm gray chalk is characteristic and has a particular beauty. It is the first of three nature drawings from the sixties in this collection (see Nos. 53 f.). Besides, there are only two or three comparable late works, plus some small sketches, and they cease altogether in Claude's last decade. Gone are the brilliant use of the wash and the daring contrasts of tone and scale of the earlier nature drawings. The late ones have a more picture-like setting, yet each carries an individual style. The purity of the means—now either pale gray tones or pen—has remained.

W 39. D 874.

47 Homage to Ceres

159 × 217 mm. Pen, brown wash, white heightening. Inscribed in the center of the verso *Claudio Gellee inventor/fecit Romae 1663.*

The subject is unique in Claude, but common to classical iconography. Ceres is leaning somewhat awkwardly on her rural throne. On the left is her carriage drawn by the traditional pair of dragons. In contrast with the preceding figure drawings, this one does not relate to another work but is an independent pictorial sheet of a characteristically narrow space. The careful execution with profuse heightening contributes to the theme of abundance. The type of image with its frontality, its horror vacui, and its stocky figures brings to mind certain engravings of the school of Raphael, which influenced

Claude also more generally in those years (cf. No. 52). To the same decade belong a few other comparable figure drawings with allegorical or mythological themes (D 879, 881, 882).

W 10. D 905.

48 Moses and the Burning Bush

194 × 225 mm. Black chalk, light gray wash. Inscribed at the bottom of the verso *Claudio Gillee/Dito il lorenese/1663 fecit*. The absurd inscription *F. PRODIGO* at the bottom of the recto and the number (?) on the right are by a later hand, probably the same as the title page of the album, around 1700 (as in No. 60).

This is the final study for the figure portion of one of Claude's major paintings (LV 161) dated a year later. The picture was commissioned by the French envoy in Rome, de Bourlemont, of Lorraine descent, who was one of Claude's important protectors. As with an increasing number of important paintings, it was painstakingly prepared by a series of drawings of the whole composition (D 921 ff.). In this detail study Moses corresponds exactly, even in size, to the painting where his pious position is, however, more convincing. The surrounding landscape is slightly modified in the interest of turning the drawing into a complete image. The pale tone and soft handling, contrasting with the vigor of earlier sheets, is characteristic of Claude's late years as is the mannerist heritage in the position and the elongation of this figure.

W 37. D 925.

49 Landscape with the Abandoned Psyche

182 × 345 mm., on two sheets joined at 105 mm. from the left. Pen, two shades of brown wash. Diagonals in red chalk. At the bottom left and right are a series of *p*'s (Claude attempting to write Psyche?), at the bottom right is *1663 Roma* (cut).

The genesis of the famous painting with Psyche in the realm of Amor after he abandoned her, later known as the "Enchanted Castle" (LV 162; 1664), can be followed over several stages. Among the studies this is the most

extraordinary. It consisted first only of the right hand sheet, which makes a complete composition based on two preceding studies (D 929f.). Claude then added the left hand sheet thereby covering up the frame line on the left side of the original sheet and, outside the frame line, the inscription *A Rome le 24* (visible when held against the light). He tested the balance of the whole by the chalk diagonals. (A vertical line near the left edge indicates a proposed reduction of the width.) The left hand design recurs independently at Oxford (D 933). For the painting Claude maintained the elongated format and the more central position of Psyche, but he straightened out the motifs of the middle ground and drew the palace of Amor in classical style. The figure is borrowed from the engraved set of Psyche, of the school of Raphael.

The verso (Pl. 64), turned sideways, contains in the lower part two parallel black chalk sketches for the classical palace façade, almost identical to the painted version. There are also two pen rectangles which correspond to the extended format of the composition. Claude experimented twice with the phrasing of a dedicatory inscription to Padre Sorba of the Collegio Romano. (The upper was the second.) Two drawings of 1664 (D 917, 927) bear the inscription.

W 45. D 931.

50 Wooded Landscape

175 × 249 mm. Pen, brown wash. On the verso are four vertical pen lines. Date: 1660–65.

The compact, surface-filling composition and the high degree of finish designate this sheet as an autonomous pictorial work. The setting is too narrow for a painting and indeed does not relate directly to any other work, but it is, in the realm of drawing, the equivalent of such paintings of densely wooded, pure landscapes as LV 163 and 166 of the mid-sixties. The view leads from the left foreground (with two female figures) over the central tree to the closed distance. The overall effect is static and symmetrical. The right edge shows a vertical sequence of framing motifs: the shrubs, the tower, the clouds, and the birds. The brilliance of early nature drawings is here replaced by a sense of solidity and a penetrating execution which unifies rather than contrasts the planes. The drawing has the marks of a work done in the studio, not in nature. Its handling, and to a large extent its type, have their analogy in the preceding and the following drawings.

W 22. D 937.

51 Landscape with Jacob at the Well

170 × 291 mm. Black chalk, pen, deep brown wash. Two sides are marked off in inches and numbered (after *10,* Claude was, as usual, in trouble). The image, indeed, measures exactly six by eleven inches *(pouces)*. On the verso the numbers are repeated, starting on the left by a sign for the first inch, followed by *1* to *10* (piercing through on the recto). The verso is also signed *Claudio Gille/fecit Roma.* Date: 1664–65.

This collection contains many of the finest preliminary studies for major paintings of Claude. The present sheet, which follows the closely comparable No. 49 by one year, is a case in point. Below the trees appear a well, flocks of sheep, and two standing women. The cover of the well is being removed by a man. This connects the drawing to one of Claude's masterpieces, the picture of Jacob, Rachel, and Leah at the well (LV 169; 1666; in the Hermitage). The drawing is the finest, the largest, and in all probability the earliest of five preliminary compositional studies. The format is that of a pair which Claude had just completed (LV 162, 167). Subsequently he was to abandon the elongated shape and to modify considerably the composition, arriving finally at an open view with a temple and one dominating central tree instead of the majestic group here. See No. 41 for the markings, No. 52 for the figures.

W 2. D 959.

52 Jacob, Rachel, and Leah at the Well

210 × 320 mm. Pen for the foreground, brown wash for the bottom, gray wash for the rest. Date: 1666.

The drawings of Esther (Nos. 41 f.) and of Jacob at the well (see the preceding sheet) are the instances in which this collection contains two kinds of preparatory studies for a painting: one of the entire composition and one of the figures. This sheet corresponds exactly, even in size, to the respective passage in the painting. At the same time, Claude turned the drawing into a self-contained image. The neat separation of the two planes according to the media is a graphic device of unfailing effect which Claude also employed elsewhere (Nos. 32, 40). As a result of the definitive execution of the design, which does not reveal any searching quality, the drawing may in theory be a copy from the finished painting (as is perhaps No. 39). But by analogy with most other figure drawings (notably Nos. 48 and 60, both of which are dated a year before their painting) this sheet was probably also done as a final preparation of the figures, at a moment when the landscape was already well advanced on the canvas. The figure group imitates Raphael's fresco of the same subject in the Vatican Loggie; the link is especially close in the two women—who occur similarly twenty years earlier in No. 18. Raphael, the inexhaustible model for every classically-minded artist, also provided inspiration for other figures by Claude (see D 725).

W 43. D 964.

53 Pastoral Landscape

177 × 235 mm. Black chalk, pen. Inscribed at the bottom center of the verso *Claudio Gillee in fect/Roma 1666.* Watermark: anchor.

The setting suggests that this drawing was done from nature. Despite its apparent simplicity, it is a work of great delicacy and technical purity. The forms are clearly determined. Three extended, parallel planes with slightly convex outlines follow each other: the bottom zone of the large plants—a device often found in Claude (see No. 37), the central platform, and the distant hills. Inserted in them are the smaller, compact shapes of the flocks (above them a herdsman is sketched in with the pencil), the trees, and the haystack which is the focal point of the whole image. The spatial progression is further emphasized by the duct of the pen, decreasing from the vigorous strokes in the foreground to the sensitive dotting manner in the distance. The formal layout resembles certain compositional drawings of the same year 1666: D 933 and 920a (Geneva), the latter showing a comparable pointillé technique.

W 17. D 955. Roethlisberger, in *Geneva,* Vol. XLI, 1968, 205.

54 *View of the Caffarella*

194 × 262 mm. Black chalk, gray wash. Inscribed at the bottom *Claud. faict* and *la chafarella. 1967*. Watermark: bird on three mounts in circle.
In the center of the image is the "casale" of the Caffarella and the valley of the same name, between Via Appia Antica and Nuova, about a mile outside Rome. Thirty years earlier Claude had often sketched in this area. It has recently become overbuilt, and its hilly character is less in evidence. This is one of the most beautiful among Claude's rare nature drawings from the late years; the same remarks that were made about the comparable No. 46 apply to it. The view, which may be compared with the less formal drawing D 841, is worked out as a pictorial image. The darker bottom zone with the pastoral scene and the lateral tree serves as a picturesque framework; clouds and birds in the sky complete the view. Within the narrow range of the gray tones Claude achieves the illusion of space by subtle gradations. The style, differing from the baroque contrasts of the earlier nature drawings, anticipates the classical trend of late seventeenth-century landscapes and of much of the following century.

W 8. D 973.

55 *St. John in the Wilderness*

220 × 201 mm. Pen, brown wash. Signed at the bottom center *Claud/fecit/ Rom*. Date: ca. 1670.
This independent drawing, though unique in some respects, may be likened to the small Magdalen of 1675 (No. 58). It is, however, somewhat larger, the motifs are grand rather than picturesque, and the handling places this work a few years earlier. The setting is entirely bound to the surface. The densely worked area of the trees contrasts with the rocky zone which consists of two repetitive sections (on the lower left is a tiny walking figure). Claude perhaps did the drawing for his nephew Jean, who had been living with him since the early sixties.
The verso (Pl. 62), turned sideways, shows a black chalk sketch of a house surrounded by a wall on the banks of a river. On the extreme left is a boat in construction; there is a touch of pen in the center. The sketch was clearly done from nature and, therefore, precedes the recto. By analogy with some

of the few other late sketches, it must date from the same time (see D 1001 v, of 1669). It represents exactly the same site as the drawing D 392, from ca. 1640, not far from Claude's home, on the left bank of the Tiber, looking downstream.

W 29. D 1023.

56 *Study for Aeneas and the Cumaean Sibyl*

193 × 245 mm. Black chalk, pen, brown wash. Inscribed at the bottom *Roma Claud. IV fecit 1669/sibilia Comana/enea*, in the four corners the four directions *mesedy, ponente, leve, tramo(nto)*; inside the image is *ischia isola, isola procida*, between the trees *bia* (for Baiae), on the right *la citta di coma*, above it *al tempo* (for tempio), and above the citadel, in chalk, *coma*; all the inscriptions were first written in chalk.
The important painting of this theme, which Claude did in 1673 for Prince Falconieri and which was last known in 1862, had a complicated start in 1669 with four drawings for a monumental setting (D 993 ff.); these were followed by a new beginning in the present work and by another, subsequent sheet (D 1062). This study is the most extraordinary of the group. It is a realistic evocation of the site of Cumae. The view is towards the southwest with Lake Averno, the Sibyl's realm, in the foreground. Claude must have known the region in his early Neapolitan sojourn, but this drawing is clearly a construction done with the help of a map, to which even the oval format may allude. Topographical accuracy also marks the painting of Egeria at Lake Nemi (LV 175), from the same year, and the *Sermon on the Mount* (D 766). For the painting of the Sibyl, Claude reverted in the end to a more majestic scenery appropriate to the subject, using, on the other hand, motifs of this drawing for the view of Delos (LV 179; 1672).

W 20. D 997.

57 *Apollo and the Muses*

216 × 583 mm. Apparently on three sheets of paper stuck together, with three vertical folds; on an old mount. Pen, brown wash, touches of white heightening in the trees. Inscribed at the bottom center *CLAVDIO. I. V. F./*

ROMA 1674, at the bottom right *CLAVD. F,* below the cartouche of Clio on the right *Claudio Gellee* (large, in chalk).

Parnassus was the subject of Claude's largest painting, done in 1652 for Cardinal-nephew Camillo Pamphili (LV 126; Edinburgh). The subject recurs thirty years later in two of his last paintings (LV 193, 195), the former of which was prepared by four elaborate drawings of 1674. In this context he also produced this large drawing, a work without peer. The figures are repeated exactly—even in size—from the respective passage of the painting from 1652 which was still in Rome (unless Claude used a preliminary drawing of 1652 which is not known to us but must surely have existed). There are a few minor changes, and the surrounding trees are adapted to the shape of the drawing. Each figure is given a didactic cartouche with the inscription of its name and attributes, copied verbatim from Cesare da Ripa's *Iconologia* (*sub* Muses). The specific purpose of the drawing escapes us. Always meticulous in mythological matters, Claude may merely have wanted to familiarize himself with the details of a particularly significant figure group in view of the new commission.

W 54. D 1070.

58 *Landscape with the Magdalen*

191 × 150 mm. Pen, brown and gray wash, some white heightening. Inscribed at the bottom left *Claudio IVF./Roma 1675.*

The penitent Magdalen is turning to the putti which appear in a cloud above her. This smallish and highly finished drawing has the pictorial character of an autonomous image; the verso shows that it was originally mounted, probably in a small frame. It repeats in greater detail and in reverse a drawing in the British Museum (D 1021) which in turn served as the study for a similar drawing of 1670 in the Louvre and bears an inscription referring to a frame. In type and mood the present drawing compares with *St. John in the Wilderness* (No. 55) and with the *Temptation of Christ* of 1676 (D 1092). The intimacy of the scene, which is limited to two surface-filling planes, echoes the art of Elsheimer and recurs within a year in a small painting, *Rest on the Flight* (LV 187).

W 1. D 1091.

59 *Landscape*

195 × 272 mm. Black chalk, light gray-brown wash, pen for the foreground and the frame. The verso, turned sideways, bears in the area of the tree a faint chalk inscription written by Claude in a very shaky hand and fully visible only on an intensified photograph: *Designe facto per il^m Principe/ Don Gaspare,* who must be Prince Altieri, for whom Claude painted in 1675 the *Landing of Aeneas* (LV 185). A comparison with dedicatory inscriptions of Claude (see D p. 54) leaves no doubt that this is a trial inscription for another, now unknown drawing (see also No. 49). Date ca. 1675.

In composition and handling this touching drawing embodies the singularly personal style of Claude's last years. A muted register of tone and delicate handling are the vehicles of a classical grandeur of vision. The composition with its great contrasts of level is typical of several of the artist's last works. Without being a study for it, the basic layout of the drawing compares with the *Landing of Aeneas* (LV 185). The distant, dominating tower on the left occurs both times, but the large river is here absent. In reverse, the drawing resembles two preliminary works for the pastoral painting LV 190, done in 1677 for Claude's most important patron, Prince Colonna. The drawing thus represents a first *pensée* for the painting, which shows a calmer scenery and pastoral figures. The reclining woman in the foreground brings to mind the abandoned Psyche or the mourning Egeria painted a few years earlier. The shaky brushwork in the central, almost dematerialized tree and the scribbling duct of the pen are attributable to the gout which, according to Baldinucci's testimony, severely incapacitated the aged artist much of the time.

W 26. D 1102.

60 *Philip Baptizing the Eunuch*

205 × 292 mm. Pen, brown wash. Inscribed at the bottom center *CLAVDIO I.V./ROMA 1677* (reinforced by Claude). The inscription *EVNVCO di CANDACE* at the bottom is by a later hand, ca. 1700 (as in No. 48).

The latest drawing of the collection is this figure study for a painting done in 1678 (LV 191: now belonging to Lord Allendale). The often encountered subject of the Apostle Philip baptizing the rich servant of Queen Candace alludes to the evangelizing activity of the patron, Cardinal Spada. Claude prepared the entire composition from a drawing of 1677 (D 1106) and probably did the present sheet as an advanced detail study when the work on the canvas was already in progress. The surrounding landscape elements, which convey a sense of great openness, are taken from the painting but adapted to the scale of the drawing. In the final version the figure group is noticeably improved and the awkward aspects of the drawing are eliminated.

W 28. D 1107.

1

2

3

4

5

6

7

8

9

34

10

11

12

13

14

15

16

17

18

19

20

22

23

24

25

28

29

30

31

33

34

35

36

37

38

daude d'oser

ti ppa fua ac quadro de princy om Aguterra
daude o mV F a

40

41

43

44

45

F. PRODIGO

48

49

50

52

53

claud fecit

la chafathal 1667.

58

59

EVNVCO DI CANDACE

5 verso

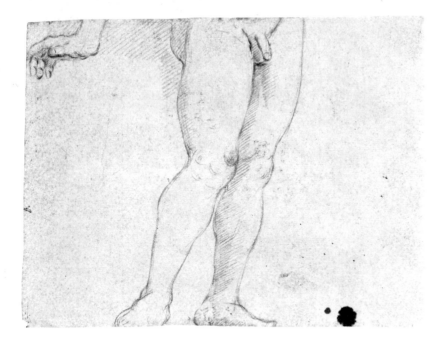

15 verso

27 verso

29 verso

61

20 verso

26 verso

34 verso

55 verso

62

17 verso

19 verso

25 verso

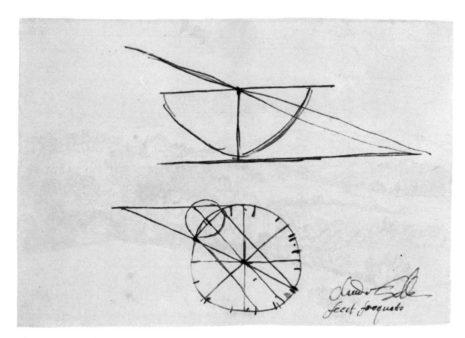

30 verso

64

Designed and printed by Conzett & Huber.
35,000 copies of this book were
printed in color gravure on 100-lb smooth-
finish gravure paper. Text was set
in Times Roman and printed in offset.
Photography is by Conzett & Huber, Zurich.